Copyright 2018 All Rights Reserved

Copyright 2018 All Rights Reserved

My Biblical Hebrew Starter Pack 2nd Edition by:
Shelby Murray Published by Biblical Languages Vocabulary, LLC

For more information and special offers visit:
www.myblv.com

www.facebook.com/biblicalhebrewvocabulary

© 2018 Shelby Murray. All rights reserved.

All rights reserved. No portion of this book may be reproduced in any form without permission from the publisher, except as permitted by U.S. copyright law. For permissions contact:

admin@myblv.com

Cover Illustration by Edwin Calderon.

Ebook Formatting by The Romanos

TABLE OF CONTENTS

SECTION	PAGE #
Introduction (no audio)	1
Basic Hebrew Grammar Rules	3
Biblical Hebrew Alphabet	5
Biblical Hebrew Vowel Points	6
Biblical Hebrew Names	8
Biblical Hebrew Names of God	10
Biblical Hebrew Vocabulary	14
Biblical Hebrew Bible Verses	44
Communion Blessings in Hebrew	46
Bonus Material:	
The Origin and Explanation of Biblical Hebrew Names (no audio)	47
About the Author (no audio)	48
Audio Files	(see page 4 for link)

Copyright 2018 All Rights Reserved

INTRODUCTION
(no audio for this page)

Shalom Friends! Let's start a journey. A journey into the incredible and fascinating world of Biblical Hebrew. What would it be like to speak the language of Adam and Eve, Moses and Joshua, King David, Daniel, Isaiah, Jeremiah, Ezekiel, and Yeshua (Jesus)? Yes Yeshua! When Yeshua told the little girl to get up, he said "Talitha Kum". (Mark 5:41) When he shouts from the stake, he says Eloi Eloi Sabachthani. (Mark 15:34) That's Hebrew friends. Hebrew is the prophesied language of **Zephaniah 3:9: "the restoration of the pure tongue so we can all worship in one accord."**

The goal of this book is to take someone with no Hebrew knowledge to a working knowledge of Hebrew in the shortest possible time. The opening pages start with the alphabet with similar sounds in English, and vowel rules, then progresses to the vowel system with examples in the English language. No prior Hebrew language training is needed. We start from the beginning, the very beginning. Then we progress to over 400 of the most common vocabulary items translated from Hebrew to English followed by the Hebrew Names of God with referenced bible verses, biblical Hebrew names, some great bible verses and finally the communion blessings in English and Hebrew. The biblical Hebrew names are a great place to start because most of the English translations of the Hebrew names are a transliteration which means the Hebrew sounds of the names are made in the equivalent English sounds. For example, Avraham translates to Abraham and similarly Dawid to David. El Shaddai is closely transliterated from Hebrew. This book contains the equivalent vocabulary of the first year of most biblical Hebrew language courses. In addition to that, we have some selected bible verses spoken in Hebrew along with the spoken Hebrew blessings for communion. Now, we can take communion the way Yeshua would by speaking the blessings in Hebrew.

Biblical Hebrew is a language much like other languages. It is best learned by engaging as many senses as possible. The senses of hearing, speaking, and seeing can be accomplished with this book. The audio file allows you to hear all the Hebrew words spoken and the translation to English. The brief pause between the Hebrew word and translation to English allows you to practice speaking. The primary method of learning in this text is visual and listening to the audio files. The Hebrew text here is a large font to allow for quick visual recognition. The biblical Hebrew vocabulary acquisition is a task that will need to be repeated many times for all the vocabulary to be memorized. But, it's undoubtedly worth the effort.

(INTRODUCTION)
(no audio for this page)

The Hebrew language when written is primarily made up of consonants. The vowels are mostly written above and below the consonants.

What if English used the Hebrew system?
What would English look like?

With vowel points: wht wld nglsh lk lk?
                                       a   ou   e   i   oo ie

Without vowel points: wht wld nglsh lk lk?

If we took out the vowels from the English language the amount of letters and pages would be greatly reduced. With a little practice, we would quickly get used to it.

BASIC HEBREW GRAMMAR RULES
(no audio for this page)

1. Hebrew is written and read from right to left. This is opposite from English.

2. There are no small case or capital letters in Biblical Hebrew. All letters are the same case.

3. Biblical Hebrew letters are printed. There is no cursive in the bible.

4. Each letter of the Hebrew alphabet stands alone. Unlike English, no letters of the Hebrew alphabet are joined together. Sounds such as 'gr' or 'fr' as in grapefruit, 'st' as in step, 'pr' as in problem.   These combinations of sounds don't exist in Hebrew.

5. Six consonants ב, ג, ד, כ, פ, ת are commonly called begadkephat, an acronym. Are used with and without a dot. This dot is called a dagesh. Today there is little to no difference in the ג and ד with and without a dot (dagesh).

בּ makes b sound ב (without dagesh) makes v sound.

תּ makes t sound ת (without dagesh) makes t or th sound.

פּ makes p sound פ (without dagesh) makes f sound.

כּ makes kh sound like bach

כ without dagesh makes a softer k sound.

However, it is very common today for many people to pronounce the תּ and ת with and without dagesh as t as in tom.

(BASIC HEBREW GRAMMAR RULES)
(no audio for this page)

What are gutturals?

Gutturals are sounds that rarely, if ever, occur in English. א, ה, ח, ע, and ר are pronounced from the back of the throat. This sounds very different to Americans and Europeans at first. The best place to start understanding might be to just listen to the audio.

א is called a glottal stop as in the initial sound of apple. When it appears at the beginning of a word, it can only be pronounced with the accompanying vowel sound. א is silent many times in the middle and at the end of words. ח (khet) and כ (khaf) might be the most difficult sounds for English speakers. These are sounds produced by friction between the back of the tongue and the soft palate. These two letters are basically the same sound in Hebrew. This might best best be learned by listening to the audio files.

Syllabification

1. Every syllable must begin with a consonant and have only one vowel.

2. Open syllables end with a vowel and closed syllables end with a consonant. Examples are noted throughout the book. This is best understood by seeing examples.

Audio Files
myblv.com/audio/hebrew
password: yood

Copyright 2018 All Rights Reserved

BIBLICAL HEBREW ALPHABET

Hebrew Letter	Transliteration	Example in English	Hebrew Letter	Transliteration	Example in English
א	aleph *(silent without an accompanying vowel)*	(a as in apple)	מ/ם	mem / final mem *(at the beginning and middle of words / at the end of words)*	(m as in mary)
ב	bet	(b as in boy)	נ/ן	nun / final nun *(at the end of words)*	(n as in new)
ג	gee-mel	(g as in girl)	ס	samekh	(s as in sierra)
ד	dalet	(d as in dog)	ע	ayin *(silent without an accompanying vowel)*	(I as in eye)
ה	hey	(h as in horse)	פ/ף	pey / final pey *(at the beginning and middle of words / at the end of words)*	(p as in peter)
ו	vav or waw	(v as in vase)	צ/ץ	tsadee / final tsadee *(at the beginning and middle of words / at the end of words)*	(ts as in pizza)
ז	zayin	(z as in zebra)	ק	koof *(soft k sound)*	(k as in king)
ח	khet *(hard k sound)*	(k as in hokma)	ר	resh	(r as in roger)
ט	tet	(t as in tango)	שׂ	seen *(notice dot on left)*	(s as in sierra)
י	yood *(English usually translates this as j)*	(y as in young)	שׁ	sheen *(notice dot on the right)*	(sh as in sugar)
כ/ך	khaf / final khaf *(hard k sound) (at the beginning and middle of words / at the end of words)*	(k as in kesef)	ת	tav	(t as in tango)
ל	lamed	(l as in lincoln)			

Copyright 2018 All Rights Reserved

BIBLICAL HEBREW VOWEL POINTS

Vowel Name	Example	Sound
Qamets	אָ	a as in yacht (long vowel)
Patach	שַׁ	a as in bat (short vowel)
Chateph Patach	אֲ	a as in bat (reduced vowel makes quick sound)
Qamets Hey	וָה	a as in yacht (long vowel)
Tsere	קֵ	a as in eight
Seghol	גֶ	e as in better
Chateph Seghol	אֱ	e as in metallic
Tsere Yod	הֵי	a as in eight
Seghol Yod	גֶי	e as in better
Chireq	עִ	e as in machine
Chireq Yod	עִי	e as in machine
Cholem	אֹ	o as in home

Annotations:
- Qamets: "Vowel Point" arrow
- Patach: "sh" pointing to שׁ
- Seghol Yod: "vowel sound" and "consonants" labels

Copyright 2018 All Rights Reserved

BIBLICAL HEBREW VOWEL POINTS

Vowel Name	Example	Sound
Qamets Chatuph	אָ	o as in home
Chateph Qamets	קֳ	bo as in bottle
Cholem Vav	וֹ	o as in home *(long vowel)*
Qibbuts	אֻ *3 dots written diagonally left*	oo as in boo *(Aleph is silent here)*
Shureq	וּ	oo as in boo *(vav consonant is silent here)*
Sheva *(or shewa)*	בְ	makes short sound of letter *can be silent or vocal*

Vocal shewa:
1. occurs at the beginning of word
2. Beginning of syllable following a closed syllable
3. Following a long vowel

Silent shewa:
1. Distinguishes the consonant as vowelless
2. Occurs in closed syllables and at the end of words

BIBLICAL HEBREW NAMES

אָדָם	(Ah-dahm)	Adam	אֶפְרַיִם	(Ef-ry-eem)	Ephraim
אַבְשָׁלוֹם	(Av-sah-Lom)	Absalom	מְנַשֶּׁה	(M-nash-she)	Manasseh
אַבְרָהָם	(Av-rah-ham)	Abraham	כֹּרֶשׁ	(Kho-resh)	Cyrus
שָׂרָה	(Sah-rah)	Sarah	מִיכָאֵל	(Mee-khah-ale)	Michael
יְרוּשָׁלַיִם	(Y-roo-shah-layim)	Jerusalem	גַּבְרִיאֵל	(Gav-Ree-ale)	Gabriel
מִצְרַיִם	(Mits-ry-eem)	Egypt	מַלְכִּי־צֶדֶק	(Mal-khee-tsedek)	Melchizedek
מֹשֶׁה	(Mo-sheh)	Moses	נֹחַ	(No-okh)	Noah
פַּרְעֹה	(Par-o)	Pharaoh	יְהוָה	(Y-ho-vah)	Yahweh or Jehovah
רָחֵל	(Rah-khel)	Rachel	אֱלֹהִים	(Eh-low-heem)	Gods
לֵאָה	(Lay-ah)	Leah	אֵל	(Ale)	God

diphthong combination of vowels pronounced together

(BIBLICAL HEBREW NAMES)

יַעֲקֹב	(Yah-ah-kov)	Jacob	יִשָּׂשכָר	(Yees-sah-khar)	Issachar
יִשְׂרָאֵל	(Yees-rah-ale)	Israel	דָּן	(Don)	Dan
רְאוּבֵן	(R-oo-vane)	Reuben	גָּד	(God)	Gad
שִׁמְעוֹן	(Sheem-own)	Simeon	אָשֵׁר	(Ah-sher)	Asher
לֵוִי	(Lay-vee)	Levi	נַפְתָּלִי	(Naph-tah-lee)	Naphtali
יְהוּדָה	(Y-hoo-dah)	Judah	יוֹסֵף	(Yo-safe)	Joseph
זְבוּלֻן	(Z-voo-loon)	Zebulun	בִּנְיָמִין	(Bean-yah-meen)	Benjamín

BIBLICAL HEBREW NAMES OF GOD

יְהוָה אֱלֹהִים	(Y-ho-vah Eh-low-heem)	Yehovah Elohim "Lord God" (Genesis 2:4)
אֶהְיֶה אֲשֶׁר אֶהְיֶה	(Eh-h-yeh ah-sher eh-h-yeh)	I am that I am (Exodus 3:14)
יָהּ *(the dot here is called a mappiq vocalizing the h sound)*	(Yah)	God (Exodus 15:2)
יְהוִה אֲדֹנָי חֵילִי	(Y-ho-vee a-do-ny khay-lee)	The Lord is my strength (Habbakuk 3:19)
יְהוָה בּוֹרֵא קְצוֹת הָאָרֶץ	(Y-ho-vah bo-ray k-tsoth hah-ah-rets)	Yahweh is creator of the ends of the earth (Isaiah 40:28)
יְהוָה יִרְאֶה	(Y-ho-vah year-eh)	Yehovah is the one that provides Jehovah Jireh (Genesis 22:13-14)
אֵל שַׁדַּי	(Ale Shad-die)	El Shaddai (Genesis 17:1, 35:11)
יהוה צְבָאוֹת	(Y-ho-vah ts-vah-oath)	Lord of Hosts (1 Samuel 1:3, Isaiah 47:4)
יְהוָה עֶזְרֵנוּ	(Y-ho-vah ez-ray-noo)	God is our help (Psalms 33:20)
יְהוָה אֱלֹהֵי הָעִבְרִיִּים	(Y-ho-vah eh-low-hey hah-eve-rayim)	Lord God of the Hebrews (Exodus 3:18)

Copyright 2018 All Rights Reserved

(BIBLICAL HEBREW NAMES OF GOD)

אֵל גְּמֻלוֹת	(Ale g-moo-loath)	The Lord of Recompense (Jeremiah 51:56)
אֵל עֶלְיוֹן	(Ale el-yone)	God Most High (Genesis 14:19)
יְהוָה שָׁמָּה	(Y-ho-vah shah-mah) *dagesh forte, doubles the mem sound*	Yahweh is present (Ezekiel 48:35)
יְהוָה יִמְלֹךְ	(Y-ho-vah yeem-loakh)	Yahweh will reign (Exodus 15:18)
יְהוָה צִדְקֵנוּ	(Y-ho-vah tsid-kay-noo)	The Lord our righteousness (Jeremiah 23:6)
יְהוָה רֹעִי	(Y-ho-vah row-ee)	The Lord is my shepherd (Psalms 23:1)
יְהוָה מוֹשִׁיעֵךְ וְגֹאֲלֵךְ	(Y-ho-vah Mow-shee-akhe v-go-ah-lakhe)	Yehovah is our savior and redeemer (Isaiah 49:26)
אֲבִיר יַעֲקֹב	(Ah-veer yah-ah-cove)	mighty one of Jacob (Isaiah 49:26)

11

Copyright 2018 All Rights Reserved

(BIBLICAL HEBREW NAMES OF GOD)

יְהוָה אֱלֹהֵי יִשְׂרָאֵל	(Y-ho-vah e-low-hey yees-rah-ale)	The Lord God of Israel (1 Kings 8:23, Psalms 106:48)
יְהוָה אֱלֹהֶיךָ אֵל קַנָּא	(Y-ho-vah e-low-heh-khah ale kah-nah)	The Lord your God is a jealous God (Deut. 5:9)
יְהוָה עֻזִּי וּמָגִנִּי	(Y-ho-vah oo-zee oo-mah-geen-nee)	Yahweh is my strength and shield (Psalms 28:7)
יְהוָה מַכֶּה	(Y-ho-vah mokh-kheh)	Yahweh is the one who strikes (Lamentations 28:7)
יְהוָה אוֹרִי	(Y-ho-vah o-ree)	Yahweh is my light (Psalms 27:1)
יְהוָה רֹפְאֶךָ	(Y-ho-vah rofe-eh-khah)	Yahweh is your healer (Exodus 15:26)
יְהוָה שָׁלוֹם	(Y-ho-vah shah-lome)	Yahweh is peace (Judges 6:24)
יְהוָה שֹׁפְטֵנוּ	(Y-ho-vah shofe-tay-noo)	Yahweh is our judge (Isaiah 33:22)

(BIBLICAL HEBREW NAMES OF GOD)

יְהוָה שֹׁפְטֵנוּ   (Y-ho-vah shofe-tay-noo)   Yahweh is our judge (Isaiah 33:22)

יְהוָה מְחֹקְקֵנוּ   (Y-ho-vah m-khoke-kay-noo)   Yahweh is our lawgiver (Isaiah 33:22)
literally, Yahweh is the lawgiver of ours

יְהוָה מַלְכֵּנוּ   (Y-ho-vah mal-khay-noo)   Yahweh is our king (Isaiah 33:22)
literally, Yahweh is the king of ours

נִבְרְכָה לִפְנֵי־יְהוָה עֹשֵׂנוּ׃   (Neev-r-khah leaf-nay y-ho-vah o-say-noo)   We kneel before Yehovah our maker (Psalms 95:6)

יְהוָה נִסִּי   (Y-ho-vah niece-see)   The Lord is my banner (Exodus 17:15)

Hebrew vocabulary beginning with the letter "aleph" with English translation

א

when accent mark is not shown it's understood to be on the last syllable

אֶ֫רֶץ	(e-rets)	land, earth, ground	אֵשׁ	(eish)	fire
אֱלֹהִים	(eh-low-heem)	God, gods	אַחַר	(ah-khar)	after, behind
אָב	(ahv)	father, ancestor	אַחֲרֵי	(ah-kha-ray)	after, behind

hateph patach, makes a reduced vowel sound

אֵל	(ale)	God, god	אֵת / אֶת־	(et/eth)	with, beside, not translated
אֲדֹנָי	(a-do-ny)	Lord	אֶל	(el)	to, toward, in, into
אָדוֹן	(ah-done)	lord, master	אֶחָד	(eh-khad)	one
אָח	(akh)	brother	אֹ֫הֶל	(o-hel)	tent
אַחִים	(ah-kheem)	brothers	אַחֵר	(ah-khare)	other, another, foreign
אִישׁ	(eesh)	man, husband	אֵיךְ	(akhe)	how?
אֲנָשִׁים	(ah-nah-sheem)	men	אוֹ	(oh)	or
אִשָּׁה	(eesh-shah)	woman, wife	אֶ֫לֶף	(eh-leph)	thousand

#

read from right to left ←   read from left to right →

אִין	(ayn)	there is not, there are not	אָהַב	(ah-hahv)	to love
אַף	(ahph)	nostril, nose; anger	אָסַף	(ah-sahf)	to gather, to take away, to destroy
אֲשֶׁר	(ah-sher)	who, whom, that, which	אָחַז	(ah-khaz)	to seize, grasp, take
אֶבֶן	(eh-ven)	stone	אָרַר	(ah-rar)	to curse
אֲדָמָה	(a-dah-mah)	ground, land, earth	אוֹר	(oar)	light, daylight, sunshine
אֹיֵב	(oy-yave)	enemy	אָמַן	(ah-mahn)	to be reliable, be faithful
אַמָּה	(ah-mah)	cubit, forearm	אָסַר	(ah-sar)	to tie, bind, fetter, imprison
אֵם	(aim)	mother	אֶרֶז	(eh-rez)	cedar
אָכַל	(ah-khahl)	to eat, consume	אָוֶן	(ah-ven)	iniquity, wickedness, evildoer
אָמַר	(ah-mar)	to say, mention, think	אוֹצָר	(oats-tsar)	treasure, treasury, storehouse
אָבַד	(ah-vahd)	to perish, vanish, become lost	אוֹת	(oath)	sign, mark, pledge

"bet"

ב

בֵּן	(bane)	son	בְּרִית	(b-reet)	covenant
בַּיִת	(bayith)	house, household	בֶּגֶד	(beh-ged)	clothing, garment
בַּת	(bot)	daughter	בָּנָה	(bah-nah)	to build
בָּנוֹת	(bah-noathe)	daughters	בָּעַר	(bah-ar)	to burn, consume
בֵּין	(bane)	between	בָּחַר	(bah-khar)	to choose, test, examine

K O T B – english consonants

בְּתוֹךְ	(b-tokhe)	in the midst of	בִּין	(bean)	to understand, perceive, consider

makes ee sound

בֹּקֶר	(bo-kare)	morning	בָּטַח	(bah-tokh)	to trust, to rely upon
בָּקָר	(bah-kar)	cattle, herd	בָּכָה	(bah-khah)	to weep
בְּרָכָה	(b-rah-khah)	blessing, gift	בּוֹשׁ	(boshe)	to be ashamed

dagesh in beit makes the b sound

בָּשָׂר	(bah-sar)	flesh, meat, skin

ב

בְּכוֹר	(b-khor)	firstborn	בַּרְזֶל	(bar-zel)	iron
בָּקַשׁ	(bah-kosh)	to seek, to search for, to demand	בָּרַךְ	(bah-rokh)	to bless
בֶּטֶן	(beh-ten)	belly, stomach, womb	בְּרֵאשִׁית	(b-ray-sheet)	in a beginning "Genesis"

aleph is silent without vowel

"gee-mel"

ג

גּוֹי	(goy)	nation, people	גָּמָל	(gah-mahl)	camel
גָּדוֹל	(gah-dole)	great, big, large	גֶּבֶר	(geh-ver)	warrior, mighty man
גַּם	(gahm)	also, even	גַּן	(gahn)	garden
גְּבוּל	(g-vool)	border, boundary, territory	גנב	(gah-nahv)	to steal

beit without dagesh makes v sound

גָּלָה	(gah-lah)	to uncover, reveal, disclose	גָּד	(god)	Gad
גָּדַל	(gah-dahl)	great, to become great	גּוֹרָל	(go-rahl)	destiny
גּוּר	(goor)	to dwell as a foreigner	גֶּפֶן	(geh-fen)	vine
גֵּר	(gare)	stranger, sojourner, alien	גֶּשֶׁם	(geh-shem)	rain

"dalet"

ד

דָּבָר	(dah-vahr)	word, matter, thing	דּוֹר	(door)	generation
דֶּרֶךְ	(deh-rekh)	way, road, journey	דֶּלֶת	(de-let)	door
דָּם	(dahm)	blood	דְּבַשׁ	(d-vash)	honey
דָּבַר	(dah-vahr)	to speak	דּוֹד	(dode)	uncle
דָּרַשׁ	(dah-rash)	to seek, to ask for	דַּל	(dahl)	poor, weak, needy

"hey"
ה

הַר	(har)	mountain, hill, hill country	הָיָה	(hay-yah)	to be, become, happen, occur
הָרִים	(ha-reem)	mountains	הָלַךְ	(hah-lokh)	to go or to walk
הֵיכָל	(hey-khal)	temple, palace	הָרַג	(ha-rahg)	to kill, slay
הֲ	(hah)	interrogative particle	הָלַל	(hah-lahl)	to praise, sing hallelujah
הֵן	(hane)	behold! if	הַלְלוּיָהּ	(hahl-l-loo-yah)	hallelujah
הִנֵּה	(hee-nay)	behold!	הֶבֶל	(heh-vel)	vanity, futility, breath

Copyright 2018 All Rights Reserved

"vav"

ו   *most common Hebrew word occurs over 50,000 times in the Hebrew Bible*

וְ	(v)	and, but, also, even
וָו	(vav)	a nail, tent peg, or hook
וַיִּקְרָא	(vay-yee-krah)	and he called or and he proclaimed
וַיֹּאמֶר	(vay-o-mare)	and he said

Leviticus 1:1

"zayin"

זָהָב	(zah-hahv)	gold	זָנָה	(zah-nah)	to commit fornication
זָקֵן	(zah-kane)	adjective: old, noun: elder	זָבַח	(zah-vokh)	to slaughter, sacrifice
זֶרַע	(zeh-rah)	seed, offspring, descendants	זֶה	(zeh)	this (masculine)
זָכַר	(zah-khar)	to remember	זֹאת	(zot)	this (feminine)
זָקֵן	(zah-kane)	to become old	זַיִת	(zayit)	olive
זָעַק	(zah-okh)	to cry out, call for help	זוּר	(zoor)	stranger, foreigner

Copyright 2018 All Rights Reserved

"khet"

ח

חַי	(khaiy)	living, alive	חֵמָה	(khay-mah)	wrath, heat, poison
חַיִּים	(khaiy-yeem)	life, lifetime	חֲצִי	(khats-tsee)	half, middle
חָכָם	(khah-kham)	wise, skillful, experienced	חָרָה	(khah-rah)	to become angry
חַטָּאת	(khah-tahth)	sin, sin offering *(aleph silent because it has no vowel)*	חָזָה	(khah-zah)	to see, behold, perceive
חַיִל	(khaiyil)	strength, wealth, army	חָלָה	(khah-lah)	to become weak or sick
חֶסֶד	(khesed)	loyalty, faithfulness	חָנַן	(khah-nahn)	to show favor or grace
חֹדֶשׁ	(kho-desh)	month, new moon	חַיָּה	(khay-yah)	animal, beast
חָזַק	(khha-zock)	to become strong	חֵלֶב	(khe-lev)	fat;
חָטָא	(khah-tah)	sin, to commit a sin	חֲמוֹר	(kh-more)	donkey *(hateph pathach very similar to shewa)*
חָפֵץ	(khah-phatse)	to take delight in	חֶרְפָּה	(kher-pah)	reproach, disgrace, shame

Copyright 2018 All Rights Reserved

"tet"

טָבַח	(tah-bokh)	to slaughter	טַל	(tal)	dew
טַבַּעַת	(tah-bah-ahth)	ring	טָמֵא	(tah-may)	unclean
טָהוֹר	(tah-hore)	pure	טַף	(tof)	children
טוֹב	(tove)	good or to be good			

"yood"

י

יוֹם	(yome)	day		יָשַׁב	(yah-shahv)	to sit, to dwell
יִשְׂרָאֵל	(yees-rah-ale)	Israel		יָרֵא	(yah-ray)	to fear, to be afraid
יְרוּשָׁלַיִם	(y-roo-shah-layim)	Jerusalem		יָרַד	(yah-rod)	to go down, to descend
יְהוָה	(y-ho-vah)	Yahweh, Lord		יָלַד	(yah-lod)	to bring forth, bear
יֶלֶד	(ye-led)	child, boy, youth		יָכֹל	(yah-khol)	to be able
יָפֶה	(yah-feh)	beautiful		יָסַף	(yah-sof)	to add, continue
יָשָׁר	(yah-shar)	upright, just		יָרַשׁ	(yah-rosh)	to inherit
יֵשׁ	(yashe)	there is, there are		יַחְדָּו	(yokh-dow)	together, at the same time
יָד	(yod)	hand; side, power		יֹחַד	(yoh-khod)	together, along with
יָצָא	(yats-tsah)	to go out, to come out		יַיִן	(ya-yeen)	wine

י

יָמִין	(yah-meen)	right hand, south	יָתַר	(yah-tar)	to be left over, to remain
יָטַב	(yah-tav)	to be well, to be pleasing	יָדָה	(yah-dah)	to thank, to praise
יָשַׁע	(yah-shah)	to be delivered	יָעַץ	(yah-atz)	to advise, to counsel

"khaf"

כ

כֹּהֵן	(kho-hane)	priest	כֹּחַ	(kho-okh)	strength, power
כֶּסֶף	(khe-sef)	silver, money	כּוּן	(khoon)	to be established
כֹּה	(kho)	thus, so	כָּסָה	(khah-sah)	to cover, to hide, to clothe
כְּ	(kh)	as, like, according to	כָּנָף	(khah-nof)	wing, edge, extremity
כֹּל	(khole)	all, each, every	כְּרוּב	(kh-roov)	cherub
כֵּן	(khane)	so, thus	כֶּרֶם	(kheh-rem)	vineyard
כַּאֲשֶׁר	(kh-ah-sher)	as, like, when	כְּסִיל	(kh-seal)	fool, shameless person
כִּי	(khee)	that, because, but, except	כָּבוֹד	(khah-vode)	glory, splendor, honor,
כָּרַת	(kha-raht)	to cut, to make a covenant	כָּבֵד	(khah-vade)	to be heavy, to be honored
כָּפַר	(khah-far)	to cover, atone, to atone	כְּלִי	(kh-lee)	vessel, weapon
כָּלָה	(khah-lah)	to be complete, to be finished, come to an end	כָּתַב	(khah-tahv)	to write, to record

Copyright 2018 All Rights Reserved

"lamed"

לֵב	(lave)	heart, mind, will	לָכֵן	(lah-khane)	therefore
לֵבָב	(lay-vav)	heart, mind, will	לֹא	(lo)	no, not
לִפְנֵי	(leef-nay)	before, in front of	לָקַח	(lah-kokh)	to take, grasp, capture, seize
לְ	(l)	to, toward, for	לָבַשׁ	(lah-vash)	to put on a garment, to be clothed
לְמַעַן	(l-mah-ahn)	on account of, for the sake of	לָשׁוֹן	(lah-shone)	tongue, language
לָכֵן	(lah-khane)	therefore	לָחַם	(la-khom)	to fight, do battle with
לֶחֶם	(leh-khem)	bread, food	לָמַד	(lah-mahd)	to learn, to teach
לְבַד	(l-vahd)	alone, by oneself	לִין	(lean)	to remain overnight
לָבָן	(lah-vahn)	white	לָמָה	(lah-mah)	why?

"mem"

מ

מֹשֶׁה	(mo-sheh)	Moses	מָלֵא	(mah-lay)	to be full, fill
מֶלֶךְ	(meh-lekh)	king, ruler	מָלוֹךְ	(mah-lokh)	to become king, to rule
מַיִם	(mayim)	water	מָצָא	(mah-tzah)	to find out, reach, obtain
מִשְׁפָּט	(mish-pot)	judgment, decision, law	מוּת	(mooth)	to die
מִזְבֵּחַ	(miz-bay-okh)	altar	מִסְפָּר	(mis-par)	number
מִן / מִן־	(mean)	from, out of	מְלָאכָה	(m-lah-ah-khah)	work, occupation, service
מַעַל	(mah-ahl)	above, upward, on top of	מִשְׁכָּן	(mish-khahn)	dwelling place, tabernacle
מִמַּעַל	(meem-m-ahl)	from above	מָלַט	(mah-lot)	to escape, flee to safety
מִצְוָה	(mitz-vah)	commandment	מִגְרָשׁ	(mig-rahsh)	open land, pasture
מִצְוֹת	(mitz-vothe)	commandments	מַמְלָכָה	(mahm-lah-khah)	kingdom, dominion, reign
מְאֹד	(m-ode)	very, exceedingly	מָהַר	(mah-har)	to hasten, to hurry
מְעַט	(m-aht)	little, few	מָכַר	(mah-khar)	to sell, hand over

Copyright 2018 All Rights Reserved

מ

מַדּוּעַ	(mah-doo-ah)	why?	מָשַׁח	(mah-shokh)	to smear, anoint
מִי	(mee)	who?	מָשִׁיחַ	(mah-shee-okh)	anointed one, Messiah
מִשְׁפָּחָה	(mish-pah-khah)	family, clan	מַלְכוּת	(mal-khooth)	kingdom, dominion
מִלְחָמָה	(mil-khah-mah)	war, battle, struggle	מִקְנֶה	(mik-heh)	cattle, livestock, property
מָוֶת	(mah-veth)	death	מִשְׁמֶרֶת	(mish-me-reth)	watch, guard, responsibility
מַטֶּה	(maht-teh)	staff, rod, tribe	מִקְדָּשׁ	(mik-dahsh)	sanctuary
מִדְבָּר	(mid-bar)	wilderness, desert, pasture	מְדִינָה	(m-dee-nah)	province
מוֹעֵד	(mo-aid)	appointed time, assembly	מַצָּה	(mats-tsah)	unleavened bread
מַחֲנֶה	(mah-kha-neh)	camp, army	מַעֲשֶׂה	(mah-ah-seh)	work, deed, act
מַלְאָךְ	(mahl-okh)	messenger, angel	מִנְחָה	(min-khah)	gift, offering, tribute

"nun"

נ

נֶפֶשׁ	(ne-fesh)	soul, life, person, neck	נָא	(nah)	please, now; surely
נָבִיא	(nah-vee)	prophet	נוּס	(noose)	to flee, escape
נָשִׁים	(nah-sheem)	women	נָגַע	(nah-gah)	to touch, strike, reach
נְאֻם	(n-oom)	utterance, declaration	נוּחַ	(noo-okh)	to rest, settle down
נַעַר	(nah-ahr)	boy, youth, servant	נָסַע	(nah-sah)	to set out, to depart
נַחֲלָה	(nah-khah-lah)	inheritance, property	נַחַל	(nah-khal)	stream, brook, wadi
נָפַל	(nah-fahl)	to fall	נָגַשׁ	(nah-gash)	to draw near, come near, approach
נָשָׂא	(nah-sah)	to lift, to raise	נְחֹשֶׁת	(n-kho-sheth)	copper, bronze
נָטָה	(nah-tah)	to spread out, to stretch out	נָשִׂיא	(nah-see)	chief, leader, prince
נֶגֶד	(ne-ged)	opposite, in front of	נָחַם	(nah-kham)	to be sorry, regret, have compassion

Copyright 2018 All Rights Reserved

נ

נָכָה	(nah-khah)	to strike, to smite, to beat, to injure	נָבַט	(nah-vat)	to look at, gaze, behold
נִצַּב	(nah-tsav)	to stand, take one's stand	נֶגֶב	(neh-gev)	south, Negev
נִצַּל	(nah-tsal)	to be rescued, be delivered	נָגַד	(nah-god)	to tell, announce, report, declare,
נָהָר	(nah-har)	river, stream	נסא	(nah-sah)	to lift up
נָבָא	(nah-vah)	to prophesy	נשק	(na-shok)	to kiss

"samekh"

ס

סוּס	(soos)	horse	סִיר	(sir)	pot
סֵפֶר	(say-fair)	book, scroll, document	סֻכָּה	(sookh-khah)	temporary dwelling
סָבִיב	(sah-veev)	around, about, surroundings	סָגַר	(sah-gar)	to shut, close
סָבַב	(sah-vahv)	to turn, to surround	סוּר	(soor)	to turn aside, turn off, leave
סמך	(sah-mokh)	to uphold, to defend	סֶלָה	(seh-lah)	selah; musical term
סָתַר	(sah-tar)	to be hidden, hide oneself			

"ayin"

ע

עֶבֶד	(e-ved)	slave, servant	עָנִי	(ah-nee)	poor, humble, afflicted
עַיִן	(ayin)	eye, spring	עַם	(ahm)	people
עִיר	(ear)	city, town	עוֹד	(ode)	again, still, as long as
עוֹלָם	(o-lahm)	forever, everlasting	עֵת	(athe)	time, point of time
עַד	(odd)	until, as far as, during	עֹלָה	(o-lah)	whole burnt offering
עַל	(ahl)	on, upon, on account of	עָלָה	(ah-lah)	to go up, ascend
עַל־דְּבַר	(ahl-d-vahr)	because of, on account of	עָבַר	(ah-vahr)	to pass over, pass through
עִם	(eem)	with, together with	עָמַד	(ah-mahd)	to stand up, take one's stand
עַתָּה	(at-tah)	now, after all, at last, then	עָנָה	(ah-nah)	to answer, testify

ע

עֲבֹדָה	(ah-vo-dah)	work, labor, service	עוֹר	(ore)	skin, hide, leather
עֲבוֹדָה	(ah-vo-dah)	work, labor, service	עֹז	(oze)	strength, power, might
עֵדָה	(ay-dah)	congregation, assembly	עֵצָה	(ayts-tsah)	counsel, plan, advice
עֶצֶם	(ets-tsem)	bone, skeleton	עוֹף	(ofe)	flying creatures, birds
עֶרֶב	(e-rev)	evening, sunset	עוּף	(oof)	to fly
עַמּוּד	(ah-mood)	pillar, column, tent pole	עָזַב	(ah-zahv)	to leave, forsake, abandon
עָנָה	(ah-nah)	to afflict, to oppress	עֶשֶׂר	(e-ser)	ten
עָזַר	(ah-zar)	to help, to assist			
עוּר	(oor)	to be awake, stir up			
עָרַךְ	(ah-rokh)	to lay out, to arrange,			

"pey"

פ

פַּרְעֹה	(par-oh)	Pharaoh	פַּר	(par)	bull, ox, steer
פֶּה	(peh)	mouth, opening	פֶּתַח	(peh-tokh)	opening, entrance, doorway
פָּנִים	(pah-neem)	face, front	פָּנָה	(pah-nah)	to turn
פְּנֵי	(p-nay)	face of	פָּתַח	(pah-tokh)	to open
פָּקַד	(pah-kad)	to attend, to appoint, to visit	פְּרִי	(p-ree)	fruit, offspring
פֹּה	(poe)	here, at this place	פָּלָא	(pah-lah)	to be wonderful
פֶּן	(pen)	lest, otherwise	פַּעַם	(pah-ahm)	foot, pace, time

Copyright 2018 All Rights Reserved

"tsadee"

צ

צָבָא	(tsah-vah)	host, army, war, service	צָרַעַת	(ts-rah-ath)	infection, disease
צְבָאוֹת	(ts-vah-oath)	Armies, Hosts	צִפּוֹר	(tsee-poor)	bird
צֹאן	(tsone)	flock of sheep and goats	צֵל	(tsale)	shadow
צְדָקָה	(ts-dah-kah)	righteousness, justice	צִוָּה	(tsah-vah)	to command
צָפוֹן	(tsah-phone)	north, northern	צָרָה	(tsah-rah)	distress, anxiety, trouble

"koof"

ק

קוֹל	(kole)	voice, sound, noise	קָבַר	(kah-vahr)	to bury
קֹדֶשׁ	(ko-desh)	holy, holiness	קָהָל	(kah-hahl)	assembly, community
קָדוֹשׁ	(kah-doshe)	holy, set apart	קָטַר	(kah-tar)	to make a sacrifice by burning
קָטֹן	(kah-tone)	small, young, insignificant	קָצֶה	(kah-tse)	end, border, outskirts
קָרוֹב	(kah-rove)	near, close	קֶדֶם	(keh-dem)	east, ancient times
קָשֶׁה	(kah-sheh)	difficult, hard, severe	קָרְבָּן	(kor-bahn)	gift, offering
קוּם	(koom)	to rise, arise, get up, stand	קֶרֶן	(keh-ren)	horn
קָרָא	(kah-rah)	to call, to proclaim	קֶשֶׁת	(keh-sheth)	bow, weapon
קָדַשׁ	(khah-dosh)	to be holy, set apart	קִיר	(kir)	wall
קָבַץ	(kah-vats)	to collect, to gather			

"resh"

ר

רֹאשׁ	(roshe)	head, top, chief
רוּחַ	(roo-okh)	spirit, wind, breath

furtive pathach pronounces the vowel before the consonant

רָחוֹק	(rah-khoke)	distant, remote, far away
רַב	(rahv)	great, many
רַע	(rah)	bad, evil, wicked
רֶשַׁע	(rah-shah)	wicked, guilty
רֶגֶל	(re-gel)	foot
רוּץ	(roots)	to run
רָעַע	(ra-ah)	to be bad, be evil, be displeasing
רֹעֶה	(roe-eh)	shepherd
רָכַב	(rah-khav)	to mount and ride, ride

רַק	(rock)	only, still, but, however
רָאָה	(rah-ah)	to see, perceive, understand

consonant is pronounced followed by vowel point

רֵעַ	(ray-ah)	friend, companion, neighbor
רָבָה	(rah-vah)	to become numerous, become great, increase
רוּם	(room)	to be high, be exalted, rise
רָעָה	(rah-ah)	to pasture, tend flocks, shepherd, feed
רָעָב	(rah-ahv)	famine, hunger
רָעֵב	(rah-ave)	[adj] hungry
רָדַף	(rah-dof)	to pursue, follow after, chase, persecute
רֶכֶב	(reh-khev)	chariot, chariot riders

Copyright 2018 All Rights Reserved

"seen"

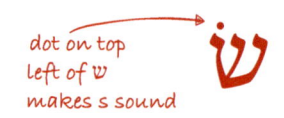

שׂ ← dot on top left of שׁ makes s sound

שַׂר	(sar)	chief official, ruler, prince	שָׂחַק	(sah-khok)	to laugh
שָׂדֶה	(sah-deh)	field, pasture land	שָׂטָן	(sah-tahn)	Satan — very close transliteration from Hebrew to English
שִׂים	(seem)	to set, to put, to place	שְׂמֹאל	(s-mole)	left side — silent vowel א with no vowel point
שָׂפָה	(sah-phah)	lip, language, edge, shore	שָׂעִיר	(sah-ear)	goat
שָׂרָף	(sah-rahf)	fiery serpent	שַׂק	(sock)	sackcloth
שָׂרַף	(sah-rahf)	to burn, destroy	שִׂמְחָה	(seem-khah)	joy, gladness
שָׂמַח	(sah-mokh)	to rejoice, be joyful	שָׂכַל	(sah-khahl)	to understand, to have success
שָׂנֵא	(sah-nay)	to hate			
שָׂבַע	(sah-vah)	to satisfy, to be satisfied			

"sheen"

שׁ ← *dot on top right of sheen makes sh sound*

שַׁעַר	(shah-ahr)	gate		שָׁמַע	(shah-mah)	to hear, understand, obey
שָׁמַיִם	(shah-mayeem)	heaven, sky		שַׁבָּת	(shah-baht)	Sabbath, period of rest

combination of vowel is a diphthong

שָׁנָה	(shah-nah)	year		שָׁכַב	(shah-khav)	to lie down with
שֵׁם	(shame)	name, reputation		שָׁלַח	(shah-lokh)	to send, stretch out
שִׁיר	(sheer)	song		שָׁמַר	(shah-mar)	to guard, keep, observe
שֶׁמֶן	(she-men)	oil, fat		שׁוּב	(shoov)	to turn back, return

vowel holem makes o sound — *makes oo sound*

שֹׁפֵט	(show-fate)	one who judges, a judge		שָׁתָה	(shah-tah)	to drink

dot on right is consonant letter "sh" sound

שָׁלוֹם	(shah-lome)	peace, welfare, wholeness		שֶׁמֶשׁ	(sheh-mesh)	sun
שָׁם	(shahm)	there, then, at that time		שָׁפַט	(shah-faht)	to judge, decide
שָׁבַת	(shah-vaht)	to stop, cease, rest		שָׁאַל	(shah-ahl)	to ask of, inquire of, request, demand

Copyright 2018 All Rights Reserved

שׁ

שֵׁבֶט	(shay-vet)	rod, staff, scepter, tribe	שִׁית	(sheeth)	to set, put, place
שָׁלֵם	(shah-lame)	to be complete, be finished	שָׁרַת	(shah-roth)	to minister, to serve
שָׁבַר	(shah-var)	to break, break in pieces, shatter	שִׁיר	(shear)	to sing
שָׁאַר	(shah-ar)	to remain, be left over, survive	שֶׁקֶר	(sheh-ker)	lie, deception, falsehood
שָׁכַן	(shah-khahn)	to settle, abide, reside, dwell, inhabit	שָׁחַט	(shah-khoth)	to slaughter
שָׁפַךְ	(shah-phokh)	to pour out, spill, shed blood	שָׁבַע	(shah-vah)	to swear, take an oath;
שָׁחַת	(shah-khoth)	to ruin, destroy, spoil, annihilate	שׁוֹר	(shore)	ox, bull, cow
שָׁמַד	(shah-mahd)	to be exterminated, be destroyed	שֻׁלְחָן	(shool-khahn)	table
שָׁמֵם	(shah-mame)	to be deserted, be uninhabited			
שָׁכַח	(shah-khokh)	to forget			

"tav"

ת

תּוֹרָה	(to-rah)	law, instruction, teaching	תּוֹעֵבָה	(to-ay-vah)	abomination, abhorrence
תַּחַת	(tah-khahth)	under, below, instead of	תּוֹדָה	(to-dah)	offering of thanks
תָּמִיד	(tah-meed)	continually	תֵּשַׁע	(tay-shah)	nine
תָּמַם	(tah-mahm)	to cease, come to an end	תְּרוּמָה	(t-roo-mah)	an offering
תָּמִים	(tah-meem)	blameless, perfect, honest	תְּרוּעָה	(t-roo-ah)	a shout of rejoicing or alarm of war
תְּפִלָּה	(t-pheel-lah)	prayer	תֵּבָה	(tay-vah)	a floating container

BIBLICAL HEBREW BIBLE VERSES

בְּרֵאשִׁית בָּרָא אֱלֹהִים אֵת הַשָּׁמַיִם וְאֵת הָאָרֶץ

Genesis 1:1
B-ray-sheet bah-rah eh-low-heem et hash-shah-mayeem v-et hah-ah-rets.
In a beginning Elohim created the heavens and the earth.

שְׁמַע יִשְׂרָאֵל יְהוָה אֱלֹהֵינוּ יְהוָה | אֶחָד

Deuteronomy 6:4 (Shema)
Sh-ma Yisra-el Yehovah Eloheinu Yehovah echad.
Hear, Understand, Obey O Israel Yehovah Eloheinu Yehovah is one.

וְאָהַבְתָּ לְרֵעֲךָ כָּמוֹךָ

Leviticus 19:18
V-ahav-ta la-ray-ah-kah kah-mo-kah
And you shall have love for your neighbor as you do for yourself.

Aaronic Blessing Numbers 6:24-26

יְבָרֶכְךָ יְהוָה וְיִשְׁמְרֶךָ

Numbers 6:24
Y-va-reh-ch-cha Yehovah v-yeesh-m-reh-cha
Yehovah bless you and keep you.

Copyright 2018 All Rights Reserved

יָאֵר יְהוָה ׀ פָּנָיו אֵלֶיךָ וִיחֻנֶּךָּ

Numbers 6:25

Ya-air Yehovah pa-nahv ay-ley-cha vee-choo-neh-ka
Yehovah cause His face to shine upon you, and favor you;

יִשָּׂא יְהוָה ׀ פָּנָיו אֵלֶיךָ וְיָשֵׂם לְךָ שָׁלוֹם

Numbers 6:26

Yee-sa Yehovah pa-nahv ay-leh-cha v-ya-same l-cha Shalom
Yehovah lift up His countenance upon you, and give you peace.

יוֹצֵר אוֹר וּבוֹרֵא חֹשֶׁךְ עֹשֶׂה שָׁלוֹם וּבוֹרֵא רָע

Isaiah 45:7

Yo-tzer -or u-voray hoshek osay sha-lom uvvoray ra.
He is forming light and creating darkness,
making well-being and creating calamity (evil).

וְשָׁמְרוּ בְנֵי־יִשְׂרָאֵל אֶת־הַשַּׁבָּת לַעֲשׂוֹת אֶת־הַשַּׁבָּת לְדֹרֹתָם בְּרִית עוֹלָם:

Exodus 31:16 (Vshamru)

V-sham-ru v-nay Yisrael et ha-Shabbat, la-sote, et ha-Shabbat, l-do-ro-tam b-rit o-lam. 16 Therefore the people of Israel shall keep the Sabbath, observing the Sabbath throughout their generations, as a covenant forever.

COMMUNION BLESSINGS

The Blessing Over The Bread:

בָּרוּךְ אַתָּה יְהוָה אֱלֹהֵינוּ מֶלֶךְ הָעוֹלָם
הַמּוֹצֵא לֶחֶם מִן־הָאָרֶץ

Barukh ata Yehovah Eloheinu melekh ha-olam hamotzi lehem min ha-aretz.
Blessed are You, Yehova, King of the universe,
who brings forth bread from the earth.

The Blessing Over the Wine:

בָּרוּךְ אַתָּה יְהוָה אֱלֹהֵינוּ מֶלֶךְ הָעוֹלָם
בּוֹרֵא פְּרִי הַגֶּפֶן

Barukh ata Yehovah Eloheinu melekh ha-olam borei p-ri hagafen.
Blessed are You, Yehovah, King of the universe, who creates the fruit of the vine

Luke 22:19 And he took bread, gave thanks and broke it, and gave it to them, saying, "This is my body given for you; do this in remembrance of me.

1 Corinthians 11:24
and when he had given thanks, he broke it and said, "This is my body, which is for you; do this in remembrance of me."

(Not read on audio)
1 Corinthians 11:26-29 26 For whenever you eat this bread and drink this cup, you proclaim the Messiah's death until he comes. 27 So then, whoever eats this bread or drinks this cup of the Messiah in an unworthy manner will be guilty of sinning against the body and blood of Yehoshua Meshiack. 28 Everyone ought to examine themselves before they eat of the bread and drink from the cup. 29 For those who eat and drink without discerning the body of Yehoshua Meshiack eats and drinks judgment upon themselves.

Copyright 2018 All Rights Reserved

THE ORIGIN AND EXPLANATION OF BIBLICAL HEBREW NAMES
(no audio for this page)

When you read the bible, have you ever wondered how did they get their names? Genesis 30:24: And she named him Joseph יוֹסֵף , for she said, "May the Lord add yet another son to my family." With only a little hebrew knowledge you can know that the name Joseph comes from the root word "yasaf" which means to add to or to continue.

Genesis 35:24 Rachel was about to die, but with her last breath she named the baby "Benoni" בֶּן-עֳנִי (which means "son of my sorrow"). The baby's father, however, called him Benjamin בִּנְיָמִין (which means "son of my right hand"). Ben simply means son of. "Ani" means sorrow or poor or afflicted and "jamin" or in hebrew "yamin" means right hand.

Genesis 14:18 And מַלְכִּי־צֶדֶק Melchizedek, the king of Salem and a priest of God Most High, brought Abram some bread and wine. "Malchi" comes from the root Melek which means king and "malchi" just means my king. "Tzedek" would be a closer Hebrew transliteration which simply means righteousness. So with just a little Hebrew knowledge we can see that Melchizedek is "My king of righteousness." Who could that be?

מִיכָאֵל Michael is made up of 3 words which are "mi" (who), "chaf" (like) and "el"(god). So Michael is "one who is like God" לֵוִי Levi is made up of "lev" (heart) and adding "hireq yod" to the ending results in "my heart". יִשְׂרָאֵל Israel is made up of יָשָׁר which means righteous or upright and אֵל which means God. Israel means "the upright of God". גַּבְרִיאֵל Gabriel is two words גֶּבֶר strong man and אֵל which means God so "strong man of God."

Many people know that Abram's name changed to Abraham and Sarai changed to Sarah. The letter hey was added to their names when God breathed into them. What many people don't know is that יוֹנָתָן Jonathan's name was changed to Johonathan יְהוֹנָתָן after he made the covenant with David. Most English translations of the bible do not note that change.

ABOUT THE AUTHOR
(no audio for this page)

My first interest in biblical Hebrew came in a bible study class on Genesis when the teacher talked about the origin of the Hebrew word for making a covenant. He said the Hebrew word is actually "carat" which means to cut. They actually would cut a covenant. There was always some kind of cutting involved. I thought why doesn't the English just translate it that way. From there, I learned more Hebrew words that I didn't think were well translated to English. So, I started searching for a biblical Hebrew class. I worked full time so seminary classes were not much of an option.

I searched biblical Hebrew on the internet and found an advertisement for an actual biblical Hebrew class at a small synagogue not far from where I worked. I called the Rabbi and asked if the class had started yet and it had but he said just to come and he would get me caught up. I remember how foreign those words looked to me when he would put them up on the overhead projector. "Devorim" (it looked so complicated) was one of our first words that had more than 3 Hebrew letters. The translation is Deuteronomy. But actually they all looked complicated at first.

Someone in the class told me that the seminary nearby had a lot of good biblical Hebrew stuff. There I found videos and a textbook. The great teacher there allowed me to sit in on one of his classes. The time made it difficult to do with my job but with prayer and the blessing of Yahweh, I was able to get through it. It would be hard for me to describe how much of a blessing and how much fulfillment I receive from studying the language of heaven: Biblical Hebrew!

OTHER BOOKS BY THE AUTHOR

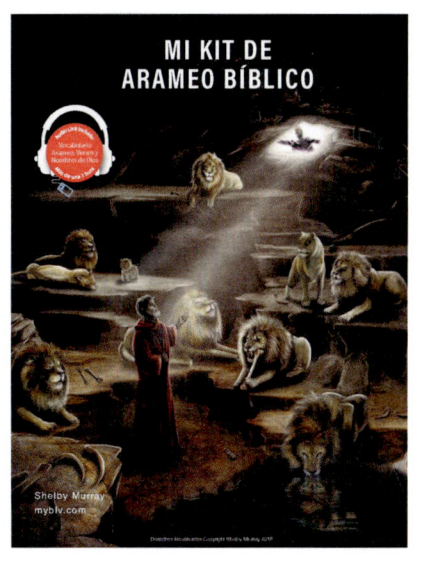

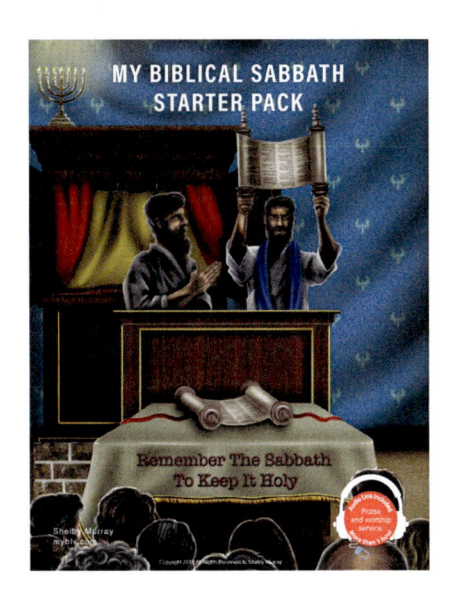

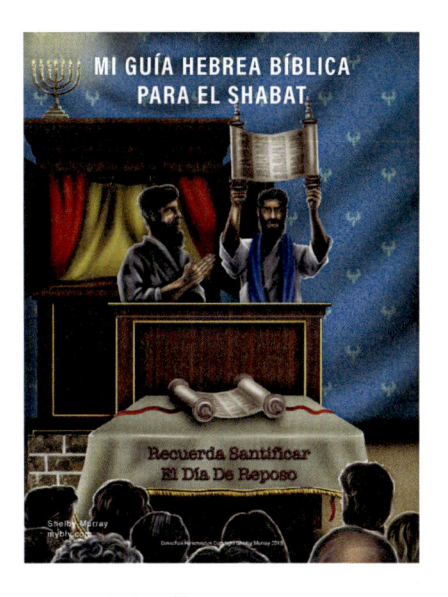

- MI KIT DE HEBREO BÍBLICO
- 我的圣经希伯来语
- MY BIBLICAL ARAMAIC STARTER PACK
- MI KIT DE ARAMEO BÍBLICO
- MY BIBLICAL SABBATH STARTER PACK
- MI GUÍA HEBREA BÍBLICA PARA EL SHABAT

visit myblv.com for special offers

Copyright 2018 All Rights Reserved

Made in the USA
Lexington, KY
22 September 2018